In Heaven's River

Poems and Carvings of Mountain-Monk

Enku

GW00567450

Translated by Julian Daizan Skinner and Sumiko Hayashi

Images by Alex Kofuu Reinke Horikitsune

Acknowledgements

Enku, the subject of this book was orphaned at age seven when his mother was drowned. All profits from this book will go to the charities, supporting the hundreds of children orphaned by the 2011 tsunami in Japan's Tohoko region. The following people have all given of their time and expertise for free:

Julian Daizan Skinner
Tsumiko Hayashi
Alex Kofuu Reinke Horikitsune

Design:
Matti Senju Sedholm
Monika Müller

Cover Design:
Astrid Baerndal

Editor (Japanese):
Noriko Yamasaki

Editor (English):
Stuart Horwitz

Proofreaders:
John Maki Evans
Justin Senryu Williams
David Bernstein
Samantha Warrington

With grateful thanks to:
Miyamae Shinzan Roshi
Ozeki Shuji
Kuze Enju Sensei
Matt Shinkai Kane
The staff of:
Seki Enku museum,
Enku Furusatokan, Minami
Senkoji, Takayama,
Nakakannondo, Hashima
Koga-jinja, Horado

Introduction

"When you look at the smile of a Buddha made by Enku, you are filled with an inexplicable warm feeling. When you see that smile, you feel happy, and when people around you look at your smiling face, they become happy too, and make other people smile. Enku Buddhas bring about such a warm feeling in people's minds. For more than 300 years, this smile has saved many people, which is shown by the fact that Enku Buddhas are still worshipped even in wayside shrines in remote areas of Japan."

Kimishige Hasegawa "Enku" (Kyosodo Shuppasha 1990)

Picture an open-faced cave in a mountain forest. In front, a stream fills the air with sounds of rushing water. This is just one of the places where I met Enku, the 17th-century Japanese wandering monk. Local tradition has it that he retreated to this cave to meditate and carve some of the 120,000 Buddha statues he had vowed to make. On his retreat he ran out of food and became too weak to descend to the village for more. So, with a prayer, he placed one of his Buddhas in the stream and waited. Sure enough, it was found in the valley below and the villagers guessed what had happened, brought him food and saved his life.

For a time, whenever I could, I'd meditate for a night or two in this cave. I would always come back down the mountain feeling like I'd been helped with my own Buddhist practice. Perhaps you have also experienced how places connected with awakened people have that enlivening quality. Many would suggest the most powerful is Bodh Gaya in India, where Shakyamuni Buddha and countless subsequent Buddhist practitioners found enlightenment. Another place that really opened me up is the sea cave on Shikoku Island where Kobo Daishi, Japan's greatest saint, realised the Way.

Since the end of the 1950s, the rough-hewn sculptures created in these wild mountain environments have exploded onto the world stage. Their maker, Enku, is probably now regarded as the most famous Japanese sculptor ever. But he was more than that. He was also an extraordinary poet who led an amazing life.

In my view he certainly imbued places with his gentle presence. But more than that, Enku appears to have had a knack of spending time in locations with a particular natural power. So it is a joy to follow his traces, and in my part of Japan, his traces are many. The most credible source has him born in 1632 on the banks of the Kisogawa, one of the great rivers of central Japan. His family was poor and, under the tightly controlled regime of the Tokugawa shoguns, there was little prospect of any kind of advancement. Social status, occupation, even religious affiliation, were rigidly prescribed. Travel was restricted.

Tradition recounts that his mother was washed away and drowned in a river flood, probably when he was seven years old. In the light of this, the team working on this book has kindly agreed to donate all profits to the hundreds of children who were orphaned during the devastating Tohoku tsunami of 2011.

Some time after losing his mother, Enku left home and became a Buddhist monk. He wrote a poem that links the two events. The emotions are all the more powerful for being unexpressed:

Waga haha no	For my mother's life
Ono chi ni kawaru	This monk's robe substitutes.
Kesa nareya	May the Dharma form
Nori no katachi wa	Continue
Yorotsuyo o hen	Ten thousand generations.

The temple Enku entered belonged to the Tendai Jimonshu, one of the older branches of Buddhism in Japan. Tendai teaching accepts many ways to realise enlightenment, including the way of the artist – the way of making and distributing Buddha statues. The Jimonshu, or Jimon branch was particularly connected with the yamabushi – literally "those who sleep in the mountains," ascetics who to this day practise while travelling along special routes and in special power spots in the wild lands of Japan.

When you begin to look at the universe through Enku's eyes, it's important to realise that, for him, the Buddhas, the Indian gods that were imported along with Buddhism, the local Japanese divinities and the Japanese emperor - in fact everybody and everything - have a place within the sphere of the divine. In Japan the word "kami", which is usually translated as "god", is not as restricted in meaning as the English connotations suggest. You and I can become kami.

Yamabushi practice blends Buddhism, Shinto and aspects of Taoism into a uniquely Japanese form. This approach found ready acceptance in the broad-based Tendai school.

Crowning the entire structure of Tendai thought is the teaching of the universalist Lotus Sutra – "Without fail, all beings will become Buddha." It was only much later in the Meiji restoration of 1868, that Buddhism and Shinto were forcibly separated. Before that, for centuries, they overlapped so much as to be in many places almost indistinguishable. So we find Enku, when he is not in the mountains, residing at Shinto shrines as often as Buddhist temples.

The first statues he seems to have made were of three Shinto gods requested by the priest of Suhara-jinja, the traditional starting point for the pilgrimage to the sacred Mount Hakusan. From this beginning, instead of the Zen injunction, "When you meet the Buddha on the road, kill him," Enku's motto could have been, "When you meet anything on the road, recognise its Buddhahood." This wonderful generosity of spirit, so present in the statues, also pours out of Enku's poems.

This generosity grew out of protracted discipline. Enku was a mountain ascetic who, in fulfilment of his vow to make 120,000 Buddha images, carved, it is estimated, about 10 statues a day. Found on the back of one of the statues is the inscription, "beggar-monk Enku" and that indicates his style of life. In common with many yamabushi, Enku was a healer and a practitioner of kampo, herbal medicine. In fact, we still possess some of his personal notes on medicinal plants. As he travelled in remote regions, his skills as a doctor would have been eagerly received among the poorer people.

So how did Enku as a Tendai yamabushi monk, actually practise? As a long-time monk myself, this question naturally came up. We don't have so much to go on in the poems themselves but I was fortunate to have had the chance to meet and learn from the yamabushi, Kuze Enju Sensei, 30th-generation descendent of Enku and current incumbent at Enku's temple, Mirokuji. When I knocked on his door and asked him to teach me how to practice like Enku, Enju Sensei took me seriously.

He explained to me how particular mountains are identified with particular mandalas or diagrams of enlightenment so that, for the yamabushi, climbing a mountain becomes literally an esoteric journey to the heart of reality. He allowed me to be present at fire ceremonies, showed me something of how a yamabushi such as Enku would have used mantras, how he would have practised identifying himself with various Buddhas and Bodhisattvas, and many other things which the traditional secrecy of the yamabushi doesn't allow me to divulge.

Embued in everything Enju Sensei taught me, was Enku's intention. "He made these statues, he lived this way, because he could see that all things, rocks, trees, pieces of wood, contain this one life, the life of Buddha, and Enku wanted everyone to feel that one life and become very happy."

In the mountains, yamabushi have two main ways to practise. Firstly they engage in pilgrimage along routes that simultaneously trace the topology of the land and the inner journey to enlightenment. Today this is generally a group practice. Secondly, yamabushi undergo solitary mountain retreats, often in caves. Enku practised both of these forms. In addition there was his carving, which was clearly a meditation for him. He was obviously successful in his practice. One poem reads:

Ureshisa wa	Joy—
Nani ni tsutsunman	Wrapping it
Kesa no sode	In my monk's robe sleeve
Kakaru tamoto wa	Hanging, full, full,
Utaka narikeri	Of joy.

One evidence of this success is the incredible energy of his life. The curator of the little museum at Enku's birthplace looked me in the eye and said, "He was a superman, you know." This superabundant energy can be seen in the enormous extent of his travels — he walked all over Japan as far as the northern island of Hokkaido, at the time almost complete wilderness, whilst carving an incredible number of Buddhas.

There is a subequent phase in yamabushi practice, and that is the return to the lowlands to work in ways that benefit others. Yamabushi acted as priests, diviners and healers. Some yamabushi were noted for digging wells or building bridges.

Periodically a yamabushi would return to the mountains to refresh his spirit so that he could descend once more renewed. In Enku's case, his sculptures linked the lowlands and the mountains. Some were presented to villagers. Others were enshrined in the heights. An eighteenth century description of Hida Province, by Hasegawa Tada describes "… caves in the high peaks or in the thick forests of the monasteries and shrines in the middle of the mountains where one finds numerous wooden Buddhas which are the work of a monk called Enku. Upon examination, however many Buddhist images there may be carved in this way in this province, one has not yet seen any that are completely finished; only the faces are there, the 'gestures of the hands' and other characteristics are indistinct, what one would usually call a sketch… one sees, nonetheless, that it is the work of an extraordinarily original hand."

Although Enku is now famous, it wasn't always this way. The above is one of the texts in which he was mentioned. Enku's life was amidst the common people. And when he was considered at all, he was thought of as a folk artist. To complete the huge number of pieces to fulfill his vow, he had to work quickly. His work concentrates on the essentials, the heart of

the piece and, for Enku, the heart of Buddhism. For him, the heart of the universe was love, radiating in a smile of pure compassion. He was an ascetic, but the rigours of his life led him into closer touch with the suffering people and simultaneously into closer touch with the bliss of enlightenment.

In his lifetime, Enku was considered an enlightened person. He was unequivocally a Budddhist monk. Probably the most recurrant word in his poems as a whole is "kesa" – a monk's robe. And yet he was also a lover, whether solely in his poems or in the fully physical sense, it is impossible to tell. He signs several of his statues, Kanki-shamon Enku, literally "Blissmonk Enku." Kankiten, the Japanese Buddhist god of sexual love and bliss, in the form of an embracing pair of elephant-headed beings, is the final statue Enku made to complete his vow. In the monastic realm, there were esoteric traditions of spiritual sexuality within the Shingon school, and also Enku's Tendai school. These schools formed an influential undercurrent throughout Japanese life, which extended even as far as the emperor's coronation ceremony. Perhaps Enku was schooled in these spiritual ways of love. His devotion to Kankiten certainly makes it possible. A friend with considerable training in Shugendo, the mountain practice approach, has raised the possibility that Enku is facing his sexuality in order to sublimate it. This is certainly possible.

Enku's poems contain none of the frank sexuality of a monastic reformer like Zen Master Ikkyu. His work is more romantic than sexual. It might be that he had romantic relationships that were nevertheless chaste. It is also possible that, when writing, he is simply adopting a literary pose. The five-line tanka form is freighted with centuries of romantic usage. Perhaps it was difficult for him to conceive of writing without including some expressions of anticipation and yearning. Whatever the truth, Enku seems quite free in recording a wide range of feeling. He writes of a former lover:

Kage utsusu	Imagining her face—
Wasuregatami mo	This memento of her
Suteyarade	I can't discard—
Kushiki no mizu o	Her make-up dish I use
Tamuku narikeri.	To offer water, praying for her safety.

11

On the other hand, he seems to have retreated to the mountains at times to purify the passions – at this time in Japan, the mountains were off-limits to women. On the festival of Tanabata, when legend relates that the stars Altair and Vega – the weaving princess and cowherd boy, joined in love for a single night of the year he wrote:

Koyoi kon	Star-lovers festival
Hito ni wa	Tonight
Awazu tanabata no	My visitor will have to wait—
Kesa no oyama ni	I'm practising up on
Machi mo koso sure.	Monk's Robe Mountain.

But not every love is correct or appropriate. In the next village to my temple in Gifu-ken in the mountains of central Japan there is a well-known hot-spring bath. Enku used to visit and would stay with the custodian's family when he did. Apparently there was a beautiful daughter of the family called Yu. It seems that Enku fell in love with her, although he kept it a secret until one morning it was discovered that he had departed, leaving in his place a statue of the young woman in the form of a nun which became a treasured family heirloom from thenceforth.

Although Enku was a prodigious traveller for the time (a contemporary book in Japanese even claims the only way he could have accomplished the amount of travelling he did was by working as a spy for the government), most of his statues have been discovered in the central area now occupied by present day Aichi-ken and Gifu-ken. This was his heartland and, you feel he knows every mountain, every village, every meditation cave. Located in the south of this area is Arako-kannon temple, now in the city of Nagoya. Here Enku carved huge nios or guardian figures that still stand in the temple gateway, as well as over a thousand koppa-butsu or "chip-buddhas", the simplest and most schematic of Enku's works, some of them practically sticks with a smile.

At the north end of Enku's home territory is Hida Senkoji. At this mountain temple too, Enku made nios for the gatway and many other statues. The priest of the temple, Shunjo, was perhaps Enku's greatest friend.

Roughly in the centre of Enku's heartland stands Suhara-jinja, a grand and imposing shrine presided over by the priestly Nishigoto family. The foundation of this shrine goes back to the climbing of Mount Hakusan, a few days walk to the north, in 717AD by a monk called Taicho. On the mountain, Taicho had visions of Buddhas and deities. A few years later, Taicho came to Suhara, enshrined Hakusan gods and appointed a member of the Nishigoto family as hereditary Shinto priest. Suhara became the starting point of an important pilgrimage route that ended on the peak of Hakusan. Enku met the 24th generation priest of the shrine, Yasu-naga Nishigoto. It seems that Nishigoto appreciated the young monk's talents and became his first patron. In Japan, where mountain reverence is embedded in the culture, almost every town seems to have its Hakusan Jinja – its Hakusan Shrine. Even Mount Fuji cannot begin to rival this level of devotion.

On the Hakusan pilgrimage route whilst meditating beneath a waterfall in June 1679, Enku had a vision of the Hakusan god coming to him and announcing, "Here lives Shaka." He was believed to have reached the same state of enlightenment as Shakyamuni Buddha, founder of the religion. From this time forward his work is considered to take on a new depth and excellence.

Not only did Enku provide spiritual solace for the people by giving away his Buddha statues and physical healing through herbal medicine, he also carried out esoteric rituals when necessary. The most famous of these was a rain ceremony in 1692 that successfully broke a drought. We have an account of it in Enku's own hand:

> Nana sai no shisha araware tama u
> Genroku go nen jinshin uzuki ju ichi nichi
> Kono reishin wa ryu o to nari
> Tennjo o ichi ji sugi o ame furu
> Dairyu no katachi wa sanjaku amari nari.
> Kono fukashigi wa daihannya o shin doku sho no toki nari Enku.

"The seven-year old messenger of the gods appeared in this world on 11th July 1692. This spiritual being is a dragon king. The dragon king crossed the sky one time and it rained heavily. The form of the dragon was more than three feet long. This mysterious event happened when Enku sincerely read and chanted the Daihannya Sutra."

This happened at Koga Jinja in Horado and seems to have been the last major public event in Enku's life. Perhaps by this time his body was wearing out from long years of travel and mountain retreats. We have a rather wistful poem referring to a mountain that rises from Koga that he'd probably effortlessly ascended many times in previous years:

Toki araba	With time
Yasuku mo noboru	Maybe I could mount the path
Miyamaji no	And master
Fukubege take no	Fukubege Mountain
Aruji narikeri.	Once again.

It seems that during this time at Koga, Enku carved his final statue – Kankiten, as mentioned above. On the base he inscribed, "Here, at this place, entering nirvana on earth." It is usual, in a Japanese context, to use the word nirvana as a synonym for death so perhaps Enku had decided that his work was done and it was time to die.

There is a persistent tradition that Enku practised mokujiki at this time - the culminating practice for one devoted to asceticism - an extremely strict vegetarian diet. Fluid intake was reduced. Pine needles, high in resin were eaten and gradually the body was dried out and permeated with pitch to the point that, after death, it would not decay and in some cases would thus be enshrined on a temple altar. The practice took a 1000 days to complete. Success was called sokushin-butsu - immediate buddhahood, and one monk who achieved this is enshrined to this day not far from Mirokuji, Enku's home temple. Other mummies of this type are found in Japan, particularly in Yamagata-ken in the north. If Enku prepared for his death in this meticulous way, you can perhaps imagine him transmitting the Dharma to his disciple, Encho, and passing away peacefully two days later on July 15th 1695. He was 64 years old. His simple grave in a beautiful bamboo grove can still be visited.

The Poems

It was Enku's thirtieth-generation successor, Enju-sensei, who gave me a copy of the collected poems and encouraged me to share them with the world. "The world loves Enku's Buddhas," he said. "Perhaps they can also love the poems."

Enku wrote prolifically. We have over 1,500 of his Japanese poems in two collections along with a few more written on the back of statues. One collection of 100 poems is called, "Kesa Niji Hyaku Shu" – "One Hundred Poems Containing the Two Characters Kesa," The other - much larger - is called "Otoko Warashi Uta", "Male Child Songs". Mostly he wrote waka (also known as "tanka"), an ancient five-line verse form with the syllables running usually, 5-7-5-7-7. We also have a few of his Chinese poems.

In the centuries preceding Enku the waka had been the verse-form of choice amongst the elite of Japan, courtiers, princes and Buddhist monks of the higher echelons. Many of the greatest poets were women and society was so permeated with poetry that a social encounter that didn't include an exchange of verses was barely imaginable. Over time, this courtly poetry became increasingly bound by rules of taste. Poems about poverty, warfare and the life of the lower classes were considered vulgar and inappropriate. Only about 2,000 words and a prescribed list of images were acceptable.

The standard collection of these elegant, urbane waka is called the Kokinwakashu. Enku is clearly familiar with it. Perhaps he studied it during his early monastery years. Later he drew on it extensively for his own poems.

It is important to realise that Enku and his society had a different conception of artistic creativity than the one prevalent in the west since the romanticism of the 19th century. An

artist joins a tradition. In his carving, each figure is clearly based in traditional Buddhist ico-
nography and yet, for the most part, unquestionably Enku's. Under his inspired chisel, the
conventionalised orthodox forms of the Buddhas and Bodhisattvas, re-emerge rough and
immediate. His poems are similarly based in a definitive source   the Kokinwakashu - and
similarly, he takes conventionalised and frequently over-refined material and transforms it
into rough, clear verses. Using a technique called "okikae uta", he would sometimes take a
whole poem and simply change a few words or a single line. This was a thoroughly accepted
mode of composition at the time. The original poem, usually one that was well known, would
stand behind the new work providing depth and resonance. Referring to all-night poetry ses-
sions, he writes of his method of composition:

Hitomoji no	Change a word—
Kawareba utano	You make a new poem.
Narumono o	Working here
Yo ni ariake no	So many times I've seen
Tsukizo hisashiki.	The moon in the dawn-light.

Let's look at one of Enku's models and the way he worked with it. This is by the great Heian
period monk-poet, Saigyo. It's hard to overstate how well-known this poem is:

Morotomo ni	Feeling this together—
Aware to omoe	Regard me with pity,
Yamazakura	Mountain cherry blossom.
Hana yori hoka ni	Flowers alone
Shiruhito mo nashi	Can understand me.

Enku takes the first line and makes:

Morotomo ni	Feeling this together:
Ukiyo no naka wa	This suffering world
Kami nareya	Is the divine world.
Omou kokoro ni	Experiencing this in your heart,
Mi wa watari tsutsu.	You can live.

So "Morotomo ni," in Saigyo's poem the expression of fellow feeling between the poet and the mountain cherry, becomes in Enku's hands the expression of the experience of the non-duality of suffering and enlightenment, this world and the transcendent – the central tenet of Mahayana Buddhism.

Comparing Enku with Saigyo, Japanese philosopher Umehara Takeshi writes, "Both Saigyo and Enku lived in the country but the orientation of their poems is 180 degrees different. Saigyo is in the country but he is always focused on the capital and concerned with recognition in the official anthologies. I read Enku's poems alongside Saigyo's Sankashu and I dare say that Enku's poems are more impressive than Saigyo's. Probably many will be unable to believe this comparison. For sure in terms of the skill of making poems, of course Saigyo is more accomplished. But Enku's poems have a higher perspective on the world. He can hear the original voice of the people and his poems about mountains and oceans have a primordial insight."

 In his life of travelling, there were a few places he returned to again and again. Chief among these is his monk friend Shunjo's temple, Senkoji. Enku presented a collection of his poems, each one containing the word "kesa", to Senkoji. He was almost obsessed, with this word, here usually translated as "monk's robe".

The kesa is a patchwork sheet worn draped over the left shoulder. Its design goes back to the time of the Buddha, who modelled it on a patchwork pattern of rice fields. In the earliest days in India, the kesa was frequently made of discarded cloth, sometimes even the wrappings of a corpse, and then dyed a muddy orange colour. In the Japan of Enku's time, gorgeous, multicoloured brocade kesas were worn by senior clerics and the rank and file wore plain black. Japanese monks, even up to today, usually wear a koromo, a Chinese-style robe with wide sleeves, and over the top, a kesa for ceremonial occasions and perhaps, for meditation.

The word kesa may have suggested a number of important connections in Enku's mind. Firstly, and most obviously, his monastic status was clearly very important to him. The overriding quality that comes through his work – writing, painting and sculpture - is utter sincerity. His life was clearly dedicated to the cause of compassion, wisdom and Buddhist enlightenment. The kesa, as the garment of The Buddha, symbolised so much of what Enku's life stood for. He frequently uses the word "kesa" as in the above poem, referring to Kesa no Yama, Monk's Robe Mountain. He constantly refers to the temple by the mountain name in his poems. Perhaps it was the site of some of his happiest times.

In addition, the poem quoted previously points to an even more intimate dimension:

Waga haha no	For my mother's life
Ono chi ni kawaru	This monk's robe substitutes.
Kesa nareya	May the Dharma form
Nori no katachi wa	Continue
Yorotsuyo o hen	Ten thousand generations.

Wrapping himself in the kesa every day and imagining that he was wrapping himself in his mother's embrace might not be so unusual. In his time many east Asian monks, like Enku, were orphans. More than that, in Enku's period the mountains, where he spent so much of his life, were considered female. Perhaps allowing yourself to experience or wrap yourself in the sacred dimension of the things around you every single day - the one great life that flows through the universe and everything in it - this is what Enku wants you to experience, so that you too can live in joy and delight, and have the generosity of heart to share it with others in your way.

Daizan
April full moon
Gyokuryuji Zen Temple
Gifu, Japan.

On Enku's trail

It was on one of our Zen mediation group meetings in my Zen master's apartment in London in spring of 2011 that we came up with the idea of this book. My publishing partner Matti Senju Sedholm was just visiting and joined me for the group meeting. The Tohoku earthquake in Japan just happened a few days earlier and we were discussing possible means to help the people affected in the catastrophic tsunami hit areas, especially the children who have lost their parents.

My master Daizan Roshi suggested publishing a translation of 100 poems of master Enku. He told us how Enku was orphaned when his mother was drowned. He showed us pictures of Enku's carvings. The simplicity of the smiles struck me first - rough pieces of wood radiating compassion.

I volunteered to take pictures for the book. Out in Japan the following spring I set off on the Enku trail. I went to his birthplace, the temple where he died and other sites connected with his life story. In all of them the great monk had left behind his unique artworks.
Nowadays Enku's figures mostly live behind protective glass. Miracle followed miracle as the staff of the various Enku consented to meeting me, handling and finally photographing these artifacts.

I am hoping I can express something of the feeling of walking into a roomful of Enku's smiles. More than that, I was allowed precious time to connect with these statues. I tried to allow each one to speak to me and these photographs are my humble attempt to respond to that communication. Sometimes the statue had me crouching or lying on the floor, sometimes closing in on a detail, even just on the wood-grain itself.

In many cases these works were carved out of firewood for poor farmers. But not only are these statues objects of worship, they are also objects of power – the power of nature, power of life, power of the enlightened spirit of Enku himself. If these pictures can convey something of the combined simplic ity and power of these statues, I will be satisfied.

On my journey, the modern-day importance of Enku dawned on me when we drove past the monument marking the very centre of Japan – a giant concrete version of one of Enku's statues emerging from the mountain foliage.

Despite this I'd been numerous times to Japan previously without hearing Enku's name. So I'm especially happy to have the chance to introduce this amazing man, his poetry and his wonderful statues to a new audience, perhaps in Japan as well as the west. My hope is that this little book will reach many people and thereby spread the word about Enku and at the same time help the orphans of the Japanese Tohoku disaster.

I am extremely grateful to all the wonderful people that made my Enku journey a huge success. Both museums and families willingly gave me permission to photograph statues. I'd particularly like to mention Mirokuji, Seki Enku museum, Enku Furusatokan, Minami, Senkoji, Takayama, Nakakannondo Hashima and Koga Jinja. I was aided and welcomed elsewhere too. I was greatly helped by my Dharma brother Matt Shinkai Kane who drove me everywhere. Thanks also to my Zen teacher Daizan Roshi and his master Shinzan Miyamae Rodaishi for their input, hospitality and help in getting me into the many different temples and museums throughout the vast area of Gifu-ken. I also owe a great debt of gratitude to Sumiko Hayashi Sensei and Mr Shuji Ozeki Sensei for their help and hospitality. And of course a big thank you to Matti Senju Sedholm for editing and designing the whole book.

Gassho Hyappai (100 bows)

Alex Kofuu Reinke

1

うれしさハ
なににつつまん
けさの袖
かかる袂は
ゆたかなりけり

Ureshisa wa
Nani ni tsutsuman
Kesa no sode
Kakaru tamoto wa
Yutaka narikeri.

Joy—
Wrapping it
In my monk's robe sleeve
Hanging, full, full,
Of joy.

2

世をのかれ
空にのほりて
在明けの
瓢ヶ岳に
出る月哉

Yo o nokare
Sora ni noborite
Ariake no
Fukube no take ni
Izuru tsuki nari.

Escaping the world
To the heavens—
Dawn
On Mount Fukebe's peak,
Late moon-sliver rising in the east.

3

七色の
花の初に
開らん
朝日に向う
玉のかつかつ

Nana iro no
Hana no hajime ni
Hirakururan
Asahi ni mukau
Tama no kazukazu.

Multicoloured flowers
Budding;
So many dewdrops
Shimmering—
Morning sunlight.

4

月の御形や
花なれや
祭るらん
浮世の罪を
きり払ひつつ

Hana nareya
Tsuki no mikage ya
Matsururan
Ukiyo no tsumi o
Kiriharaitsutsu.

Offering flowers,
Celebrating
Full moon;
Cutting-off
The suffering of our sins.

5

よろこひの
秋のも中に
作らん
世も円なる
月かとそおもふ

Yorokobi no
Aki no monaka ni
Tsukururan
Yomo madoka naru
Tsuki katozo omou

In bliss—
Autumn midnight—
Carving.
This world becomes
One full-moon circle.

6

一夜二夜
九夜十夜に
あけもせて
長き闇路に
迷ぬるかな

Hitoyo futayo
Kokonoya toya ni
Ake mo sede
Nagaki yamiji ni
Mayoi nurukana.

One night, two nights;
Nine nights, ten nights,
With no dawn.
On a long dark road
Lost.

7

水の面に
たが書おきし
面影の
君か記念と
打詠つつ

Mizu no mo ni
Ta ga kakiokishi
Omokage no
Kimi ga katami to
Uchi nagametsutsu.

Water surface.
Who drew
This face?
I stare at
Your memory.

8

法の道
鹿あふ野への
人ならは
花京も
よそに見るらん

Nori no michi
Shika au nobe no
Hito naraba
Hana no miyako mo
Yoso ni miruran.

On the Dharma way
In wild deer country;
Finding
The beauties of the capital
Here.

9

峯の松
老の形も
花なれや
雪振袖に
ちりかかりつつ

Mine no matsu
Oi no katachi mo
Hana nareya
Yuki furu sode ni
Chirikakaritsutsu.

Gnarled
Mountain-peak pines'
Flowers—
This snow held in your arms—
Like falling petals.

10

東風吹は
なひくか今日の
青楊は
春のみとりは
花の主貿

Kochi fukaba
Nabikuka kyo no
Aoyagi wa
Haru no midori wa
Hana no arujika.

East wind—
Today's floating
Willow,
So green
It overmasters even the flowers.

11

白ら山や
洲原立花
引結ふ
三世の仏の
玉かとそおもふ

Shirayama ya
Suhara Tachibana
Hikimusubu
Miyo no Hotoke no
Tama katozo omou.

Hakusan, great white mountain,
Join
Suhara and Tachibana
With snow, the Buddhas'
Treasure.

12

飛騨の国
三ツ呂の森の
霊成か
三ツ三玉の
鳥かとそ思ふ

Hida no kuni
Mitsuro no mori no
Tama naruka
Mitsumitama no
Tori katozo omou.

Up in Hida country
The spirit of the forests
Of the three regions,
This
Buddha-Dharma-Sangha bird.

13

作りおく
宮田の里の
神なれや
花の御方と
人や再拝

Tsukurioku
Miyata no sato no
Kaminareya
Hana no mikage to
Hito ya orogamu.

Made for the people
Of Miyata Village
To worship forever—
This beautiful
Divine form.

14

小坂寺
ましたの山ニ
形うつす
普すくふう
誓在せ

Osakadera
Mashita no yama ni
Kage utsusu
Amaneku suku u
Chikai Mashimase.

In Osaka Temple
On Mashita Mountain
Is a Buddha statue
Vowed
To save all beings.

15

打渡る
作る越しの
かこはしや
只ひとすしに
渡る厂かね

Uchiwataru
Tsukuru koshiji no
Kago hashiya
Tada hitosuji ni
Wataru karigane.

Crossing
The pass
In a slung basket ropeway
One line of people
Like migrating geese.

16

世の中は
いかにくるしと
思へけさ
こころの人に
かかる思ひお

Ika ni kuru shi to
Omoe kesa
Kokoro no hito ni
Kakaru omoi o.

No matter
How hard and sad
This world,
In my heart there's one
I long for.

17

白や山や
神ノ形ハ
小児なれや
白馬ニ乗て
弓矢持つつ

Shirayayama ya
Kami no mikage wa
Chigo nareya
Hakuba ni norite
Yumiya mochitsutsu.

I saw
Hakusan Mountain's
Divine form—
A child on a white horse
Holding bow and arrows.

18

飛たの国
ふる初雪は
花なれや
心の内の
春かとそ思ふ

Hida no kuni
Furu Hatsuyuki wa
Hana nareya
Kokoro no uchi no
Haru ka to zo omou.

In Hida country
First snows falling
Like blossoms.
In my heart
I feel spring.

19

ありかたや
此は神代の
言なり
心あさくは
身も荒ぬらん

Arikataya
Kore wa kamiyo no
Makoto nari
Kokoro asaku wa
Mi mo aranuran.

Even though
My heart is shallow,
Body coarse,
For this divine world,
I'm grateful

20

足からや
富士の御山の
関までも
安くも越る
鳥そらかも

Ashikara ya
Fuji no miyama no
Sekimade mo
Yasuku mo koyuru
Tori sora kamo

Ashigara,
Fuji Mountain's
High road checkpoint,
Sailing over—
Birds of the sky.

21

折かとて
武蔵の野への
糸薄き
袖打払ひ
君かくるカも

Orukatote
Musashi no nobe no
Itosusuki
Sode uchiharai
Kimi kakurukamo.

Thinking of you in Musashi's fields
Amidst tall silver grasses.
I fold my sleeves.
Will you hide there,
Or will you come?

22

松嶋や
梳器の水を
手向らん
玉よりくるか
結ふかすかす

Matsushima ya
Kushiki no mizuo
Tamukuran
Tama yori kuruka
Musubu kazu kazu.

Matsushima bay—
A water-offering
Bowl
Holding billions
Of jewels.

23

大峯や
天ノヲ川に
年をへて
又くる春に
花を見らん

Omine ya
Tenno okawa ni
Toshio hete
Mata kuruharuni
Hana o mirurun.

At Omine Mountain—
Immersed in Heaven's River
Perhaps later
I'll emerge
To view the blossoms.

24

世二伝ふ
歓喜ふ神ハ
我なれや
口より出る
玉のかつかつ

Yo ni tsutau
Yorokobu kami wa
Ware nareya
Kuchi yori izuru
Tama no kazukazu

They call me
The joyful god,
Really, me?
They say my words
Are jewels.

25

古も
今もちり行
花なれや
嵐の風に
世ハまかせつつ

Inishie mo
Ima mo chiriiku
Hana nareya
Arashi no kaze ni
Yo wa makasetsutsu.

From ancient times
Until today,
When storm winds blow
The blossoms fall—
Surrender everything to the way.

26

もろともに
浮世の中は
神なれや
思心に
身渡りつつ

Morotomo ni
Ukiyo no naka wa
Kami nareya
Omou kokoro ni
Mi wa watari tsutsu.

Feeling this together:
This suffering world
Is the divine world.
Knowing this in your heart,
You can live.

27

出いかは
千々鏡と
成玉ふ
幾万代ニ
御形のこさん

Ideikaba
Chiji no Kagami to
Naritamoo
Ikuyorozu yo ni
Mikage nokosan.

On this pilgrimage
I left thousands of statues—
Mirrors of the divine
To remain
Ten thousand generations.

28

目をふさき
月はいくつに
在物を
普く照す
心もや見ん

Me o fusagi
Tsuki wa ikutsu ni
Aru mono o
Amaneku terasu
Kokoro mo ya min.

Eyes closed
You don't see the moon everywhere,
Always shining
In your heart too.
Don't you see?

29

天地も
清御船の
池ならは
法の蓮の
世に浮ふらん

Ame tsuchi mo
Kiyoki mifune no
Ike naraba
Nori no hachisu no
Yo ni ukaburan.

If sky and earth
Form a pond
With a pure boat,
Those who realise the Dharma lotus—
Can float free.

30

清ミ濁る
世ニ浮草
絶もせて
普救
種をまきつつ

Suminigoru
Yo ni ukikusa mo
Taemosete
Amaneku sukuu
Tane o makitsutsu.

Clear and cloudy,
Always this world.
To save the people
I spread
These Buddha seeds.

31

よしあしも
をのが心の
閑なる
思ふ心に
神ぞ守る

Yoshiashi mo
Onoga kokoro no
Shizuka naru
Omou kokoro ni
kami zo mamoru.

Good, bad
Depends on your mind.
So be at peace.
If you quiet the mind
The divine will surely protect you.

32

歓喜
イツモ絶せぬ
春なれや
浮世の人を
花とこそ見れ

Yorokobi wa
Itsumo tayasenu
Haru nareya
Ukiyo no hito o
Hana to koso mire.

Delight
Like eternal
Spring;
Seeing even the suffering people
As so many flowers.

33

楽ん
心と供
法の道
月の京の
花遊賀

Tanoshiman
Kokoro to tomoni
Nori no michi
Tsuki no miyako no
Hana no asobika.

Enjoying,
Body and mind unified—
The Dharma way, feeling I'm
In the capital city of the moon
Viewing blossoms.

34

作りおく
神の御形の
円なる
浮世を照す
かがミ成けり

Tsukurioku
Kami no Mikage no
Madoka naru
Ukiyo o terasu
Kagami narikeri.

I made
These gentle
Divine figures
To be mirrors, giving light
To this suffering world.

35

法の道
御音を聞くは
ありがたや
神諸供
明ほのの空

Nori no michi
Mikoe o kikeba
Arigataya
Kami moro tomoni
Akebono no sora.

On the Dharma way
I hear the divine voice—
Overwhelming gratitude
Inspired
Beneath this dawn sky.

36

木にだにも
御形移
ありがたや
法の御声は
谷のひびきか

Ki ni dani mo
Mikage o utsusu
Arigataya
Nori ni Mikoe wa
Tani no hibiki ka.

Even trees,
Are buddha forms.
Upwelling gratitude—
The sound of the valley stream
Is the Dharma voice.

37

千和屋振る
神の祭ハ
春なれは
予行く先ハ
蓬莱の嶋

Chihayaburu
Kami no matsuri wa
Haru nareba
Waga yukusaki wa
Hourai no Shima

Now it's spring
My destination—
The spiritual festival
In the land
Of the immortals.

38

作りおく
宇賀姫神
久しきに
八百万代ノ
祝守護か

Tsukurioku
Uganohimegami
Hisashiki ni
Yaoyorozuyo no
Iwau mamorika

Made for posterity,
This Benzaiten Goddess.
Over long years and countless generations,
Please celebrate happiness,
Protect the people.

39

薬子の
法の泉を
汲上て
手に取るからに
玉の尾にせん

Kusurigo no
Nori no izumi o
Kumi agete
Te ni toru kara ni
Tama no o ni sen.

The medicine servant,
Healing Buddha's assistant—
From the Dharma fountain
Scooping
The water of salvation.

40

けさの山
上野の野へに
若なつむ
万代かけて
いわふ心か

Kesa no yama
Uwano no nobe ni
Wakanatsu mo
Yorozuyo kakete
Iwau kokoro ka.

Monk's Robe Mountain
In High Fields village,
Picking new greens.
Like this, how many generations
Have celebrated spring?

初春の
山田のあぜに
若菜摘
袖振はへて
人の来らん

Hatsu haru no
Yamadano aze ni
Wakana tsumi
Sode hurihaite
Hito no kururan.

New year
On a mountain field path
I'm picking new greens.
Coloured sleeves waving—
She's coming!

皆人ハ
仏に成と
願つつ
まことになれる
けさの杉の木

Mina hito wa
Hotoke ni naru to
Negaitsutsu
Makoto ni nareru
Kesa no suginoki.

Everyone
Wants
To become a Buddha,
But this Senkoji cedar
Can really be one!

43

深山木や
けさのおやまハ
其ままに
梅香清き
仁王成けり

Miyamagi ya
Kesa no oyama wa
Sono mama ni
Ume ga ka kiyoki
Niou narikeri

This deep forest tree
On Monk's Robe Mountain,
As it is,
Can be a sweet-scented
Buddhist guardian.

44

これやこの
くされる浮き木
とりあげて
子守の神と
我は成なり

Koreya kono
Kusareru ukigi
Toriagete
Komori no kami to
Warewa nasu nari.

Just here
Rotting
Floating wood I fished out
To make
A child-protecting Buddha.

予母の
命に代る
袈裟なれや
法の形ハ
万代へん

Waga haha no
Ono chi ni kawaru
Kesa nareya
Nori no katachi wa
Yorotsuyo o hen.

For my mother's life
This monk's robe substitutes.
May the Dharma form
Continue
Ten thousand generations.

珍しや
煎賀我屋の
土大根
稲荷の神の
守護自在

Mezurashiya
Niruka wagaya no
Tsuchidaikon
Inari no kami no
Mamori mashimasu.

How rare!
Fresh radish from my old home
Offered to Inari,
Requesting
Abundance and protection.

66

47

形移す
忘記念も
捨やらて
梳木の水を
手向成けり

Kage utsusu
Wasuregatami mo
Suteyarade
Kushiki no mizu o
Tamuku narikeri.

Imagining her face—
This memento of her
I can't discard—
Her make-up dish I use
To offer water, praying for her safety.

48

打詠ム
梳木の水ニ
残るらん
見る形たにも
忘れかたみ賀

Uchinagamu
Kushiki no mizu ni
Utsururan
Miru kage danimo
Wasuregatamika.

Blankly staring
Into the water
In her old make-up dish
Her face appears; at least
This is a memento.

49

まどひきて
位の山
登らん
心の暗に
予迷ワすな

Madohikite
Kurai no Miyama
Noboruran
Kokoro no yami ni
Ware mayowasuna.

In delusion
Climbing
Kurai Mountain
Lest I get lost in my heart's
Darkness.

50

わが恋は
玉の台に
墨染て
書文だにも
清く清らに

Waga koi wa
Tama no utenani
Sumi so mete
Kaku humi dani mo
Kioku kiyorani.

My love should be
Dyed monk's robe colour
In high places.
Even these letters I write
Should be pure.

51

関の寺
世々に目出度
皇の
龍のつかさと
いわ井そめつつ

Seki no tera
Yoyo ni medetaki
Tsumeragi no
Ryu no tsukasa to
Iwai sometsutsu.

Seki Temple
Standing through the eras
Of each august emperor.
Now the shrine of the Dragon Master
Celebration!

52

よわにきく
法の御音の
たへやらで
夜な夜な事
あらたまりぬる

Yowa ni kiku
Nori no mikoe no
Taeyara de
Yona yona kotoni
Aratamari nuru.

Heard at midnight
The Dharma-voice
Unceasing,
Night by night
Yet ever-new.

53

ミとりこハ
今日やあすやと
遊らん
宮井目出度
神かきの里

Midorigo wa
Kyo ya asu ya to
Asoburan.
Miyai medetaki
Kamikaki no sato.

Infants
Today, tomorrow
Playing around
This sublime
Village shrine.

54

松風に
袖吹払へ
小児桜
花落掛る
春の遊賀

Matsukaze ni
Sode fukiharae
Chigozakura
Hana chirikakaru
Haru no asobika.

Pine wind
Shakes your sleeves.
Tiny cherry blossoms
Fluttering—
Spring play.

55

一字の
かワれは歌と
成物を
世に在明の
月そ久しき

Hitomoji no
Kawareba utato
Narumono o
Yo ni ariake no
Tsukizo hisashiki.

Change a word—
You make a new poem.
Working here
So many times I've seen
The moon in the dawn-light.

56

こよひこん
人ニワあわす
七夕の
けさのおやまに
待もこそすれ

Koyoi kon
Hito ni wa awazu
Tanabata no
Kesa no oyama ni
Machi mo koso sure.

Star-lovers festival
Tonight
My visitor will have to wait—
I'm practising up on
Monk's Robe Mountain.

57

あかずして
別るるけさの
白玉ハ
君がかたみと
つつみてぞゆく

Akazu shite
Wakaruru kesa no
Shiratama wa
Kimi ga katamito
Tsutsumitezo yuku.

Before dawn
Parting from the shining jewel
Of Senkoji Temple—
Your memory
I wrap up and go.

58

千ハヤフル
扇は空に
円なる
照る月と
再拝みつつ

Chihayaburu
Ougi wa sora ni
Madoka naru
Teraseru tsuki to
Mata ogamitsutsu.

Divine
Skyfan
Round moon
Shining moon, once again
I bow to you.

59

おしなへて
春二あふ身の
草木まで
仏成る
山桜哉

Oshinabete
Haru ni au mi no
Kusaki made
Hotoke ni naruru
Yamazakura kana.

Everything together
Joined in spring.
Even trees and weeds
Become Buddhas
And this cherry tree is supreme.

60

幾度も
けやきの御供木
立て見よ
けさの御山の
仁王成けり

Ikutabi mo
Keyaki no misonae
Tatete miyo
Kesa no miyama no
Niou narikeri.

Many times
I stood, looked
At this sacred keyaki tree
And now it's become
Monk's Robe Temple's guardian god.

80

61

高沢や
閼伽井の水
形移す
三世仏の
鏡成けり

Takazawa ya
Akai no mizu ni
Kage utsusu
Miyo no Hotoke no
Kagami narikeri.

In Takazawa Temple
Holy water
In the sacred well—
A mirror reflecting
The Buddhas of all times.

62

駒か鼻
国見の坂の
神なれや
世の歓喜
御形成けり

Koma ga hana
Kunimi no saka no
Kami nareya
Yo no yorokobi no
Mikage narikeri

Kunimi Mountain's slope
Is the trunk—
Of the elephant god
That embodies bliss
In this world.

63

閑林独坐福峯暁
仏法僧鳥聞一鳥
一鳥一声人在心
人心般若去了々

Kanrin ni hitori zasu fuku no mine no akatsuki
Bupposo tori iccho o kiku
Iccho issei hito wa kokoro ni ari
Jinshin no hannya wa ryoryo to saru.

Quiet sitting, alone in the Fukubegatake forest,
Hearing a Buddha-Dharma-Sangha bird.
One bird, one song, in your heart—
Evil thoughts gone.

64

人住ぬ
不破の関屋の
板庇
荒にしのちハ
たゝあきの風

Hito sumanu
Fuwa no sekiya no
Itabisashi
Arenishi nochi wa
Tada aki no kaze.

No one lives now
In the checkpoint building.
Through the eaves
The autumn wind
Blows.

65

事もなき
ことをば長く
祈るなよ
いそぐ刃の
ひまを守るに

Koto mo naki
Koto oba nagaku
Inoru nayo
Isogu tsurugi no
Hima o mamoru ni.

No time to pray
For trifles,
My blade is hurrying
To carve
Universal protection.

66

立上る
天の御空り
神成か
高加山の
王かとぞ念

Tachi noboru
Tenno misorano
Kami naruka
Kouga no yama no
Ou kato zo omou.

Ascending
To the heavens—
Koga Mountain's
Divine
Dragon King.

67

幾度も
承餅は
神なるか
かつかつ守
玉のおもかな

Ikutabi mo
Tamawaru mochi wa
Kami naru ka
Katsu katsu mamoru
Tama no omo kana.

Whenever
I'm given pounded rice—
Precious, divine—
I can just about stave-off
Starvation.

68

思うてふ
草のはことに
けさの山
あきなき色に
心かけぬる

Omoucho
kusa no ha goto ni
kesa no yama
akinaki iro ni
kokoro kakenuru.

Caring about every leaf
On Monk's Robe Mountain—
Why yet
No autumn colour?
My heart frets.

69

秋風の
吹き行かたハ
けさの山
ゆふへの空の
こひしかるらん

Akikaze no
Fukiyuku kata wa
Kesa no yama
Yube no sora no
Koishi karuran.

Autumn wind
Blows
On Monk's Robe Mountain,
The evening sky
Fills me with loneliness.

70

春くれハ
消る氷ハ
けさの山
こころのひほの
我にとけなん

Haru kureba
Kiyuru koori wa
Kesa no yama
Kokoro no iho no
Ware ni tokenan.

Spring coming
On Monk's Robe Mountain.
Ice melts away;
My heart too
Melts.

71

たひながら
人の心は
暗なれや
ミしかき世々ニ
語ルマモなし

Tabi nagara
Hito no kokoro wa
Yami nareya
Mijikaki yoyo ni
Kataru mamo nashi.

On this journey
Darkness
In peoples' minds.
Life so short
And no time to talk.

72

こゑたへす
なけや鶯
けさの山
一夏来ぬる
今日をかきりに

Koe taezu
Nake ya uguisu
Kesa no yama
Hitonatsu kinuru
Kyou o kagiri ni.

On Monk's Robe Mountain
Now summer has come,
Sing, Nightingale!
Never stop!
We only have today.

73

わかれては
ほとハへたつと
けさの山
霞なからに
かかる恋しき

Wakarete wa
Hodo wa hetatsu to
Kesa no yama
Kasumi nakara ni
Kakaru koi shiki.

Time gone
Since I left
Monk's Robe Mountain
Hiding my love
In the mist.

74

身ほとを
知れは社住
つれつれの
暮す隠の
山の下庵

Mino hodo wo
Shireba koso are
Tsurezure no
Kurasu kakure no
Yama no shite iho.

Getting to know
With my body
The hidden life
Idling
In this mountain hut.

75

ほそほそと
たえすきにけり
けさの山
今日ぬぬ染る
荷糸かも

Hosobosoto
Taezu kinikeri
Kesa no yama
Kyou nuisomeru
Hasu no ito kamo.

Looping back again
To Monk's Robe Mountain—
Like a sewing thread
Making my rope
To heaven.

76

こけむしろ
筺のいわやに
しきのへて
長夜のこる
のりのとほしミ

Kokemushiro
Shou no iwaya ni
Shiki nobete
Nagaki yo nokoru
Nori no tomoshibi.

Moss carpets
Flute-sounds Cave.
Spreading through
The long night—
The Dharma light.

77

しづかなる
鷲のいわやに
住みなれて
心の内は
苔のむしろに

Shizuka naru
Washi no iwaya ni
Sumi narete
Kokoro no uchi wa
Koko no mushiro ni.

Becoming familiar
With peace
In the Cave of the Eagle;
My heart's centre,
Carpeted with moss.

78

ときハなる
色もかわらぬ
けさの山
夕部の紅葉
かすか秋風

Toki wa naru
Iro mo kawaranu
Kesa no yama
Yube no momiji
Kasu ka aki kaze.

Time passing;
Unchanging colours
On Monk's Robe Mountain.
Maple leaves in the dusk,
Quiet autumn wind.

79

しのへけさ
涼しくもあるか
夏衣
日も夕暮の
雨の名残に

Shinobe kesa
Suzushiku mo aruka
Natsugoromo
Hi mo yugure no
Ame no nagori ni.

I must endure—
Wearing a summer robe
In the chill
Of autumn twilight
After sudden rain.

80

初雪の
ふりしく時ハ
けさの山
夕部の風に
花そ散ける

Hatsuyuki no
Furishiku toki wa
Kesa no yama
Yube no kaze ni
Hana zo chirikeru.

First snow
Fallen on Monk's Robe Mountain.
Flowers upon flowers
Blown from the trees
In last night's wind.

81

年のよの
さすが蜂屋の
串の柿
蜜と見まごう
甘口こして

Toshi no yono
Sasuga Hachiya no
Kushi no kaki
Mitsu to mimagou
Amakuchi ni shite.

On new year's eve,
Eating dried persimmons
From Hachiya.
As I'd heard, sweet
As honey.

82

見るからに
遊びならも
法の道
心の春ニ
花や開らん

Meru kara ni
Asobi nara mo
Nori no michi
Kokoro no haru ni
Hana ya sakuran.

Even a playful
Glance
Into the Buddha's way
Makes your heart
Blossom.

83

千和屋振る
笙のいわやに
みそぎして
深山の神も
よろこびにけり

Chihayaburu
Sho no iwaya ni
Misogi shite
Miyama no kami mo
Yorokobi ni keri.

In the Cave of the Flute
Purifying
Myself;
Delighting
The deep forest gods.

84

色なしと
人や見るらん
けさの山
心の墨に
染てかかれは

Iro nashi to
Hitoya miruran
Kesa no yama
Kokoro no sumi ni
Somete kakareba.

Colourless—
Monk's Robe Mountain—
To those people
Who have dyed their hearts
With charcoal.

85

霞たつ
けさの山へハ
とをけれと
吹きぬ風ハ
花の香そする

Kasumi tatsu
Kesa no yama e wa
Tookeredo
Fuki nu ru kaze wa
Hana no kazo suru

Monk's Robe Mountain
Covered with mist.
Spring is far
But the wind carries the fragrance
Of flowers.

86

けさの露
心を花ニ
おきそめて
吹く風事ニ
心かけぬる

Kesa no tsuyu
Kokori hana ni
Okisomete
Fuku kaze goto ni
Kokoro kakenuru.

This morning's dew
Draws my mind
To the flower of my heart—
How fragile
In the wind!

87

白雪の
ふりてつもれる
けさの山
すむ人さへも
思ひきぬらん

Shirayuki no
Furite tsumoreru
Kesa no yama
Sumuhito sae mo
Omoikinuran.

White snow
Falling, piling-up
On Monk's Robe Mountain,
Even people who live here
Are worried.

88

飛鳥の
こゑもきこへぬ
けさの山
心のおくに
かかる人かも

Tobutori no
Koe mo kikoenu
Kesa no yama
Kokoro no oku ni
Kakaru hito kamo.

On Monk's Robe Mountain,
No birds sing.
Deep
In my heart
There's someone.

89

けさの山
嶺に分る
風雲ハ
つれなき君に
心かけぬる

Kesa no yama
Mine ni wakaruru
Kazagumo wa
Tsurenaki kimi ni
Kokoro kakenuru.

Monk's Robe Mountain peak
Dividing
The stormy clouds;
I think on
Your coldness.

90

かけ染て
法の道しも
急らん
今日立春ハ
午年哉

Kakesomete
Nori no michi shimo
Isoguran
Kyou tatsu haru wa
Uma no toshi nari.

Starting out again
On Buddha's road,
I must hurry!
Today spring starts—
Year of the horse.

91

ちわやふる
峯や深山の
草木二も
有あふ杉に
御形移さん

Chihayaburu
Mine ya miyama no
Kusaki nimo
Ariau sugi ni
Mikage utsusan.

Divine—
Mountain peak, deep forest,
Trees, weeds;
Cedars I see there
I make into Buddha statues.

92

しのぶらん
濁二染ぬ
荷はの
八重九重の
神の台か

Shinoburan
Nigori ni somanu
Hachisuha no
Yae kokonoe no
Kami no utenaka

Endurance—
The lotus flower in the mud;
Eight or nine petals, despite all
Blooming—
The divine altar.

93

御形再拝
普照す
しらさらん
浮世人ハ
おそろしや

Osoroshiya
Ukiyo no hito wa
Shirazaran
Amaneku terasu
Mikage orogamu.

Awful—
How the people in this suffering world don't see
The Buddha's aid.
Pray with gratitude, you are
Surrounded by his light.

94

覆物哉
なへて浮世を
詠れは
心の月を
普も

Amaneku mo
Kokoro no tsuki o
Nagamureba
Nabete ukiyo o
Oou mono kana.

Deeply look
Into your mind's moon,
And you can accept
The world-suffering
Covering all things.

95

音にきく
位の山の
榊はハ
手ニとる度ニ
花かとそおもふ

Oto ni kiku
Kurai no yama no
Sakakiba wa
Teni toru tabi ni
Hana ka to zo omou.

As I heard
Kurai Mountain's
Greenfresh sacred sakaki trees
Wherever you look—
Beautiful as flowers.

96

万代に
破袈裟の
衣哉
朝日ニさける
花かとそミる

Yorozuyo ni
Yabururu kesano
Koromoya
Asahini sakeru
Hanakatozo miru.

Forever thus—
Dawnlight
Through holes
In my surplice and robe
Like flowers.

97

チワヤフル
たつかとそおもふ
北の海
只ひとすじに
渡日の本

Chiwayaburu
Tatsuka tozo omou
Kita no umi
Tada hitosuji ni
Wataru hi no hon.

On sacred peak
Stood, contemplating
The northern sea
I've one thought—
The Rising Sun Country I've trekked up.

98

伊福山
法ノ泉の
湧出る
水汲玉ノ
神かとそ思ふ

Ibukiyama
Nori no izumi no
Waki izuru
Mizu kumu tama no
Kami ka to zo omou

On Mount Ibuki
The wellspring of the Dharma
Emerges—
I scoop divine
Water-Jewels.

99

時在は
安々登る
ミ山路の
福部嶽
主なりけり

Toki araba
Yasuku mo noboru
Miyamaji no
Fukube ga take no
Aruji narikeri.

With time
Maybe I could still mount the path
And master
Fukube Mountain
Once again.

100

老ぬれは
残れる春の
花なるか
世に荘厳き
遊ふ文章

Oe nureba
Nokureru haru no
Hana naru ka
Yo ni kedakake ki
Asobu tamazusa.

Getting older
How many more springs?
How many more flowers?
Seriouly
I play with these phrases.

Afterword

In May 2012, after completing the work on these poems, I placed a copy on Enku's grave at Mirokuji, and then walked with a Zen friend for several days amidst the mountains up the valley of the Nagara River past Enku's birthplace, past Suhara-jinja, where his first statues were enshrined, and then the waterfall where he realised enlightenment and finishing at the gateway temple to Hakusan, White Mountain, the great holy peak of central Japan.

We left a copy of the poems on the mountain altar with the following poem inscribed in it:

May these leaves
flutter
all over this world-mountain,
spreading Enku's joy
where they land.

Notes on the Poems

2. Fukube is a small mountain rising from Koga Jinja in Gifu-ken, a shrine where Enku lived for some time towards the end of his life. The peak of Fukube gives spectacular views of Hakusan and Ontake, the two great sacred mountains of central Japan.

5. Not only is the full moon a popular symbol for enlightenment, but "en" the first character of Enku's name has the meaning of round, fullness or completion. (It is the same character as that used for "yen", Japanese money)

6. Enku's poem on the dark night of the soul that so many spiritual seekers have to pass through on their way to enlightenment.

7. Commentators believe the face is that of a former lover, or that of Enku's mother, who was washed away in a river flood when the boy was seven years old.

11. Shirayama, or as it is more popularly known, Hakusan, is the great mountain of central Japan. It can easily stake a claim to being the most revered mountain in Japan if judged by the huge number of Hakusan shrines found throughout the country. Enku has a special connection with Hakusan.

The mountain was first opened in 718 C.E. by a charismatic monk named Taicho. On the three main peaks Taicho had visions of Buddhas and Bodhisattvas. The mountain quickly became a place of pilgrimage. The three peaks, Gozen-ga mine (2702m), Onanji-ga mine (2684m) and Ken-ga-mine (2680m) were seen as the sources of three great rivers, Tedori-kawa, Kuzuryu-gawa and Nagara-gawa, which flow out to irrigate the three surrounding provinces.

The original gods of the mountain came to be seen as Buddhas appearing in a form that the Japanese people could relate to and respect. Thus Shinto and Buddhism were conflated. Taicho brought the ancient Nishigoto family of Shinto priests to Suhara Jinja, a shrine he opened in the valley of the Nagara River south of Hakusan. Suhara became the starting point of one of the three pilgrimage routes to Hakusan.

Tachibana is another important point on this route. The Nishigoto Yasunaga, 24th priest in the lineage was Enku's first patron. The statues of Shinto gods that he commissioned are still enshrined in Shinmei-jinja, Minamai-shi and revered to this day.

12. Hida is the old name for a mountainous region in the north of Gifu-ken. The Bupposo bird or Buddha-Dharma-Sangha bird, gets its name from the sound of its call.

13. Miyata village is in the mountains of northern Gifu-ken.

14. This refers to Osaka village in Hida, not the city in Kansai. The temple he is referring to is called Chokokuji. In Enku's time and down to the present day, particular statues of Buddhas and Bodhisattvas were attributed particular powers. Some of his own statues are associated with such beliefs. For example, in Hoonji temple in Ogaki, Gifu-ken and Ongakuji temple, Konan, Aichi-ken both have carvings of Yakushi nyorai, the Buddha of healing, together with his 12 guardian assistants. Sick villagers would borrow the guardian associated with their time of birth and enshrine it by their sick bed, worshipping it until health was restored.

15. Enku is referring to a rope bridge in the mountains where travellers were slung in a basket beneath the rope and pulled across the gorge. There were several of these on the borders of Hida and Ecchu (now Toyama) during Enku's time.

17. A visionary poem. The monk Taicho, (682-767), founder of the Hakusan Shinko – the Hakusan faith – was a spiritual child prodigy. From the age of 14, he lived in a cave on Mount Chizon in Echizen (now Fukui). Here Enku sees the Hakusan god in the form of Taicho on a white horse holding bow and arrows – traditionally associated with the piercing insight that penetrates to the heart of things.

Another time, while performing waterfall immersion practice, Enku received a vision of the Hakusan god who announced, "You sit where the Buddha sits." In other words, you have realised Buddhahood.

20. Travel in Enku's time, was heavily restricted and travellers had to pass through many checkpoints. Ashigara, close to Hakone and south of Mount Fuji, was famous as it was surrounded by steep cliffs.

21. A love poem. Musashi was famous for its susuki – silver grass. These grasses are used for offerings at the viewing of the great autumn full moon. The poem thus contains an autumnal association.

22. Matsushima, a bay famous for its islands and pine trees. Counted as one of the three most beautiful sights of Japan. When the great haiku poet, Basho, saw the bay studded with pine, his effusion runs: "Matsushima, ah! Matsushima! Matsushima!"
Basho and Enku were contemporaries although of rather different social classes. Although there is no historical evidence for it happening, when the Japanese television station NKT screened a dramatisation of Enku's life, it included a meeting of the two poets.

23. The Omine range in Nara Prefecture is the most sacred place for yamabushi practice. There is a pilgrimage route that runs through the range, taking about ten days. Enku practised in a cave in Omine over the winter of 1675-76 and probably wrote this waka at that time. Tenkawa, Heaven's River, runs at the foot of the range, but in this poem Enku seems to be using the river as an image for his immersion in meditation. The earliest chronicle of Japan constantly speaks of the deities meeting together "in a divine assembly in the bed of the tranquil river of heaven", so Enku is immersed in a place where he can encounter the divine.

26. Enku borrows from a poem by Saigo found in the Kokinwakashu, the standard waka collection:

Morotomo ni	Feeling this together–
Aware to omoe	Think of me with pity
Yamazakura	Mountain cherry blossom.
Hana yori hoka ni	Flowers alone
Shiruhito mo nashi	Can understand me.

30. The Buddha seeds that Enku spreads are his statues.

33. An indirect reference to an old folktale called Takeori Monogatori. A poor childless couple find a beautiful baby inside a bamboo. They take care of her and she grows into a beautiful young woman. Three aristocratic suitors come seeking her hand. She sets each of them a test, but they all fail. On one full moon night she tells the elderly couple that it is time for her to return home and she disappears to the moon, where all is beautiful.

37. Enku wrote this poem, radiant with enlightenment after leaving his winter retreat cave on Omine. Horai no Shima is the mythical Isle of the Sennin, the immortals.

38. Benzaiten is the Japanese form of the Indian goddess, Saraswati. Already known in Japan in the sixth century, she is the only female member of a popular (and rather miscellaneous) group of deities called the seven lucky gods. She is considered the goddess of eloquence and creativity.

39. Yakushi nyorai, the Buddha of healing is depicted along with twelve assistants. In this poem, Enku is ambiguous as to whether he is referring to the healing work of one of these assistants or to a human healer carrying out Yakushi's work in this world. In common with many yamabushi, Enku was a healer. We still have some of his notes on the healing properties of various plants. The Healing Buddha Sutra, along with many Buddhist teachings, points out that the true medicine is the Dharma. The water or elixir of the Dharma, kanro in Japanese, amrta in Sanskrit, has many parallels with the ancient Greek ambrosia – the sustenance of the gods.

42. A gentle joke in the original. Enku, of course, is about to transform the tree into a Buddha. He refers to the tree again in the next poem. In Senkoji, Enku made two huge guardian statues for the temple gate, using whole trees. One of the most famous images of Enku, found in the "Kinsei-kijen-den", "Traditions relating to Extraordinary persons of Recent Centuries" by Ban Kokei, illustrates this feat.

44. Concerning this poem, Kuze Enju Sensei, Enku's Dharma descendent and current priest of Mirokuji, wrote "Enku created a poem featuring a female form of Bishamonten, the protector of children, Kishibojin (also written Kariteibo in the scriptures). Kariteibo had many children, some sources indicated five hundred, one thousand or even ten thousand. Nevertheless, everyday she killed people's children and ate them. When the Buddha discovered the way Kariteibo scorned the people and behaved so cruelly, he hid her beloved youngest child, Piyankara. In this way the Buddha made her realise how devastated people were when they lost their children. The contrite Kariteibo made a confession and repented and resolved from thenceforward to protect people's children and take refuge in Buddha's teaching. The iconic form of Kariteibo always has some children playing around her knees and her body is voluptuous. She is considered the goddess of safe delivery and protector of children."

45. Enku's grief over the untimely death for his mother, and gratitude for her life led him to build a small temple in his birthplace, Takega-hana, centred on a magnificent statue of Kannon, embodiment of compassion.

46. Perhaps on a visit back to his birthplace, Enku wrote this poem, celebrating the daikon, the large radish that forms a significant part of the rural Japanese diet even to this day. Inari is the Japanese god of the harvest.

49. Mountain practice was a means of purification for Enku. Kurai no Yama in central Gifuken is the mountain where Jimmu Tenno, the mythical first Emperor arrived after his descent from the "high plains of heaven".

51. When he was 57 years old, Enku restored Mirokuji temple on the banks of the Nagara River in Seki. Although it's history was long, standing through the reigns of many emperors, the temple had been abandoned. Enku refers to himself in this poem as "Ryu no tsukasa", dragon controller or dragon intermediary—one who can operate in the human world and also in the spiritual world of the dragons.

55. Enku's composition style illustrated here. Using the technique of okikae uta – taking a previously written poem and re-writing it in a way that enough of the original remains to provide depth and resonance to the new poem. Only about 100 poems out of his total output of around 1500, have no relation to previous poems.

56. To this day, Tanabata, the star festival is considered the most romantic night in the Japanese calendar. Based on a Chinese legend of a weaving princess and her cowherd lover, the stars Altair and Vega, the story goes that their love-making together was so delightful and consuming that they neglected their work. The order came from heaven that they were to be separated either side of the River of Heaven (the Milky Way). Only once a year, on the night of Tanabata could they cross the river and meet each other. Basho captures the atmosphere:

Fumi-zuki ya	Night before
Muika mo tsune no	The lovers' meet—
Yo niwa nizu.	Air of anticipation.

Enku's perspective is different. In the Edo period, women were not allowed into the mountains. On his Tanabata night, his lover will have to wait. His mountain practice comes first.

57. Enku's farewell to "his only friend on earth", Shunjo, the Abbot of Senkoji Temple on Monk's Robe Mountain.

59. Written on the back of a famous statue of The Bodhisattva of Compassion he made from cherry wood and enshrined in Kannon-do, Ibuki-shi, Shiga Prefecture.

61. Almost a thousand years old, Takazawa Temple is situated on the mountain behind my temple. To this day a sacred spring arises behind the Hondo, the main Buddha Hall and flows beneath it. People come from long distances to collect and drink the healing waters.

62. A poem about Kunimi Mountain in Gifu-ken, the slope of which looks like an elephant's trunk. This created an association between the mountain and the deity Kankiten. Kanki – bliss, Ten – god; the most overtly tantric of the Buddhist images occurring in Japan, the iconic form is of two elephant-headed human figures embracing. Enku's connection with Kankiten is shown in a number of ways. Sometimes he signed his name, Kanki Shamon Enku – Bliss Monk Enku. The last statue he ever made was a Kankiten figure, now to be seen at Koga-jinja in Gifu-ken. Here he celebrates "the god that embodies bliss in this world." As well as the esoteric Kankiten practices involving the transmutation of sexual energy to spiritual bliss, ordinary people have been going to the god for centuries to pray for good marriages and for children.

63. One of Enku's few Chinese poems.

65. Enku's view on the spiritual purpose of his carving.

66. This poem commemorates Enku's successful rain-making ceremony. The introduction contains Enku's inscription memorialising the event.

67. Pounded rice, mochi, is a highly concentrated food. For someone constantly on the edge of survival, it takes on a wondrous quality.

76-77, 83. Retreat poems from Mount Omine, the heartland of yamabushi training.

81. Hachiya is in present day Mino Kamo, southern Gifu-ken, an area still noted for its persimmons

95. The evergreen leaves of the sakaki tree are used as offerings on Buddhist and Shinto altars to this day. Kurai Mountain in Gifu-ken is the place where Jimmu Tenno, the mythological first Emperor of Japan descended from the heavens in a boat.

98. Ibukiyama is the mountain on which Enku began his yamabushi mountain practice. There is an Enku statue enshrined on the summit to this day.

99. Fukube Mountain is situated behind Koga Jinja, a shrine in a beautiful peaceful valley. Enku lived here towards the end of his life and in a time of drought performed his successful rain ceremony at which the assembled people saw a dragon in the sky. It seems that the ceremony probably exhausted Enku as soon afterwards he returned to Mirokuji, the temple he restored, to die. The frailty and exhaustion of a monk who has spent his life in arduous spiritual practice is highlighted when you realise that Fukebe mountain is very easy to climb. To reach the top only takes an hour or so from Koga Jinja.

100. Believed to have been written when he was about sixty years old and near the end of his life. Still his experience of enlightenment, his feeling of spring, continues; and with it the ability to smile at his "serious" playing.

Notes on the Images

Page 23. Kongodoji; Dharma-protecting deity.

Page 25. Shinto Deity. Although a Buddhist monk, Enku's work was never circumscribed. He belonged to a branch of the Tendai School, whose all-embracing worldview contained an extraordinary pantheon of figures. Enku's carving career began with the Shinto gods of Suhara Jinja in the Nagaragawa river valley and he often returned to Shinto figures.

Page 27. Buddha's hand. The varada mudra symbolises generosity.

Page 29. Yakushi Nyorai, The Buddha of Healing. One of Enku's most common subjects; sometimes he includes the twelve attendants of this trans-historical Buddha.

Page 31. The smile. "For more than 300 years, this smile has saved many people, which is proved by the fact that Enku Buddhas are deified and worshipped even in wayside shrines in remote corners of Japan." From "Life of Enku," Kimishige Hasegawa.

Page 33. Fudo Myo O; the embodiment of steadfastness and immovability. From the Heian period (794-1185) onwards, Fudo became a central image in Shugendo, the ascetic mountain-practice branch of Buddhism to which Enku belonged.

Page 35. Kojin – god of the kitchen fire, sometimes claimed to be a self-portrait.

Page 37. Bodhisattvas (literally bodhi – awakening, sattva – being). Beings dedicated to awakening both themselves and others.

Page 39. "...even though you do not have money or things, you can make a great offering. The first offering is a gentle look, the second is a peaceful face, a face filled with joy; a face which makes other people happy and gives hope to people. It is this teaching that must have been embodied in the faces of Enku Buddhas." From "Life of Enku," Kimishige Hasegawa. Kongodoji, normally depicted as a wrathful figure.

Page 41. Arhat Binzuru (Sanskrit: Pindola). Arhats are enlightened students of the Buddha. Binzuru is believed to have been requested by the Buddha to remain in the world. As in this example, statues of him are frequently well-worn, since the faithful follow the custom of rubbing a part of the statue corresponding to the sick parts of their bodies, as he is reputed to have the gift of healing.

Page 43. One of the many forms of Kannon, the Bodhisattva of Compassion.

Page 45. Detail of Ryomen Sukuna, a deity connected with the foundation of the province of Hida where Enku spent much time. There is also a connection with healing – significant for Enku who was expert in herbal medicine.

Page 47. Kongo Rikishi. One of a pair of fierce nio, temple gate guardians. The nio, whose form is likely influenced by the Hellenistic Heracles, demonstrate how no aspect of humanity is inherently evil, even aggression finding its value in protecting the truth. This figure with his mouth closed is called Ungyo ("Un-form"), and embodies the end of all things.

Page 49. Eleven-headed Kannon. Popular in the Esoteric or tantric versions of Buddhism, the eleven-headed Kannon was one of Enku's favorite subjects. Kannon is the Bodhisattva or embodiment of compassion and often has a feminine appearance. The eleven heads are said to have occurred when Kannon witnessed the suffering of all beings. Because of her intense desire to help in all directions, her head split into eleven pieces.

Page 51. Buddha in meditation; looking down, inwards and yet outwards with infinite tenderness.

Page 53. Amida mudra detail; the so-called Mida-no Jouin Mudra The right palm is placed over the left with three fingers extended. Two circles are formed with index fingers held together with the tips of both thumbs. The right hand represents enlightenment. The left hand represents the world of appearance—or illusions. This mudra symbolises the triumph of enlightenment over the world of illusions.

Page 55. Arhat; one of the original enlightened followers of Buddha tasked to remain in the world helping all beings.

Page 57. Fudo Myo O, embodiment of immovability holding the sword that cuts through delusion.

Page 59. Daikokuten, literally the 'great black god', one of the seven Japanese gods of good fortune. He is traditionally shown corpulent and standing in barrels of rice and is associated with the kitchen and prosperity in the household.

Page 61. Bodhisattva. Enku's smile of blessing over all living beings.

Page 63. Bodhisattvas. At times Enku's work was highly finished. Other times he worked fast and simply - this process leading to his famous "koppa butsu" or "wood-chip buddhas". One of Enku's modern devotees once said to me wonderingly, "He saw everything as a potential Buddha."

Page 65. Eleven-faced Kannon, the embodiment of compassion. Found at one of the two possible birthplaces of Enku, tradition has it that he created this very figure in memory of his mother who had been washed away in a river flood leaving him an orphan.

Page 67. Bodhisattva.

Page 69. Enku's Bodhisattva smile over all beings.

Page 71. Bodhisattva robe detail showing Enku's simple and strong chisel lines.

Page 73. Amida. "there is not the slightest differentiation as to whether one is a layman, monk, male, or female... after believing with deep conviction that it is the Primal Vow of Amida Tathagata that delivers all hopeless beings of weak capacity." Rennyo Shonin (1415-1499), a great teacher of faith in Amida who had taught in Enku's area.

Page 75. Fudo; his determination and engagement highlighted by wrinkled brow and staring eyes.

Page 77. Zenzai doji, the archetypical Buddhist pilgrim journeying towards enlightenment in the Kegon Kyo.

Page 79. Amida Buddha, the Buddha of Infinite Light (or Infinite Life). A trans-historical figure who vowed to meet each of his devotees at the time of death and conduct them to his pure land – a place ideally suited for realising liberation. Faith in Amida is the most popular form of Buddhism in Japan. Advances in modern medicine have led to an ever-increasing number of people who have been technically dead for some period and then returned. Accounts of these near-death experiences have shown staggering commonalities. Returnees often report being met and guided by a figure of light.

Page 81. Shinto god

Page 83. Shinto god

Page 85. Fudo detail.

Page 87. Bodhisattva detail

Page 89. Eleven-headed Kannon. Lit, 'Regarder of the cries of the world.' Embodiment of compassion.

Page 91. Hachiman Kojin Eight-Headed Earth God.

Page 93. Shinto god

About the Translators

Julian Daizan Skinner Roshi is the first Englishman to go to Japan and become a full Zen Master in the rigorous Rinzai School. He received Dharma Transmission in the Soto Manzan Lineage from Daishin Morgan Roshi and in the Zendo Kyodan Inzan lineage from Shinzan Miyamae Roshi of Gyokuryuji in central Japan. A former pharmaceuticals industry scientist, twenty-five years ago Daizan Roshi gave up his job, sold his house, gave all the money away and became a Zen monk. A published poet, Daizan Roshi has also made a study of the shugendo, mountain-practice tradition, including consulting with Kuze Enju Sensei – twentieth generation spiritual descendent of Enku and current incumbent of Mirokuji – the temple Enku restored at the end of his life, and with Zen teacher and yamabushi, Donin Okuda Sensei.

Sumiko Hayashi is a translator and former teacher. Sumiko's Buddhist studies began at an early age. She first encountered Enku after she married. The couple moved into a house next door to Nyoiji Temple, Ginan-cho, Gifu-ken. The temple enshrines several Enku statues. Sumiko continues to study and practice Buddhism and yoga.

About the Photographer

Alex Kofuu Reinke Horikitsune was for a long time the only European taken on as a traditional Japanese craft family apprentice by the world famous irezumi artist Horioshi III in Yokahama. Today he is Horioshi's senior apprentice. Interested in Zen and Japanese culture since his early teens, Horikitsune formally took the Zen precepts with Daizan Roshi in 2011. His Zen study continues. Together with his business partner Matti Senju Sedholm Horimatsu, Horikitsune established book publishers, Kofuu-Senju Publications, and has supplied photography for several books.